INSTAGRAM FOR BEGINNER AND INTERMEDIATE USERS

-How to use the app, take great pictures and grow your following without buying ads!

Intro

Hello and welcome to my Ebook! This book is about the app Instagram: what it is, how it works, and how to gain meaningful followers. This book is for beginner and intermediate users. It is perfect for small business owners, young entrepreneurs or people who just want to connect with others! If you are already familiar with the app, feel free to skip the next section on Instagram basics.

Why am I an expert on this topic? Why should you listen to me? For one, I have been using Instagram for many years, and I was able to gain more than 1800+ followers quickly, organically and with little effort. Also, I have a degree in photojournalism and another in sociology. I wrote my sociology thesis on Instagram, focusing on why people post. After writing 8000+ words for my thesis, I learned tons of useful information about the platform. Most of all, I like to do things cheaply and easily, and the great thing about Instagram is that you do not need lots of time or money to achieve success.

My Experience with Instagram

I signed up for Instagram around 2018 with the name: 'unfiltered_photography_' and began to post pictures. In the beginning I posted photos from my archive, as I worked as a photojournalist for a few years in my past. I had thousands of photos in my archives, so I did not have to continuously create content, which is a great strategy when starting out. Creating content takes effort and time, so fortunately I did not have to worry about that aspect in the beginning.

Once I started using the app, I began to wonder, how easy is it to get followers? I started practicing the techniques that I outline in this book, and my page started growing! After a few weeks, I was inspired to start shooting new content and I settled on having street photography/documentary photography as my theme. I found other Instagram users with the same vision and style, and after a few months I hit the milestone of 1000 followers! Yes it took some time to interact with others and to get people to notice my page, but I was consistent. I continue to use Instagram regularly, so please read this book with confidence! The main strategy that I will show you is how to meet people and how to get them to notice your page. I have tons of experience with this app, so much that I felt like I was getting addicted. Therefore, please read all of my disclaimers that pop up in this book, as these apps are addictive by design.

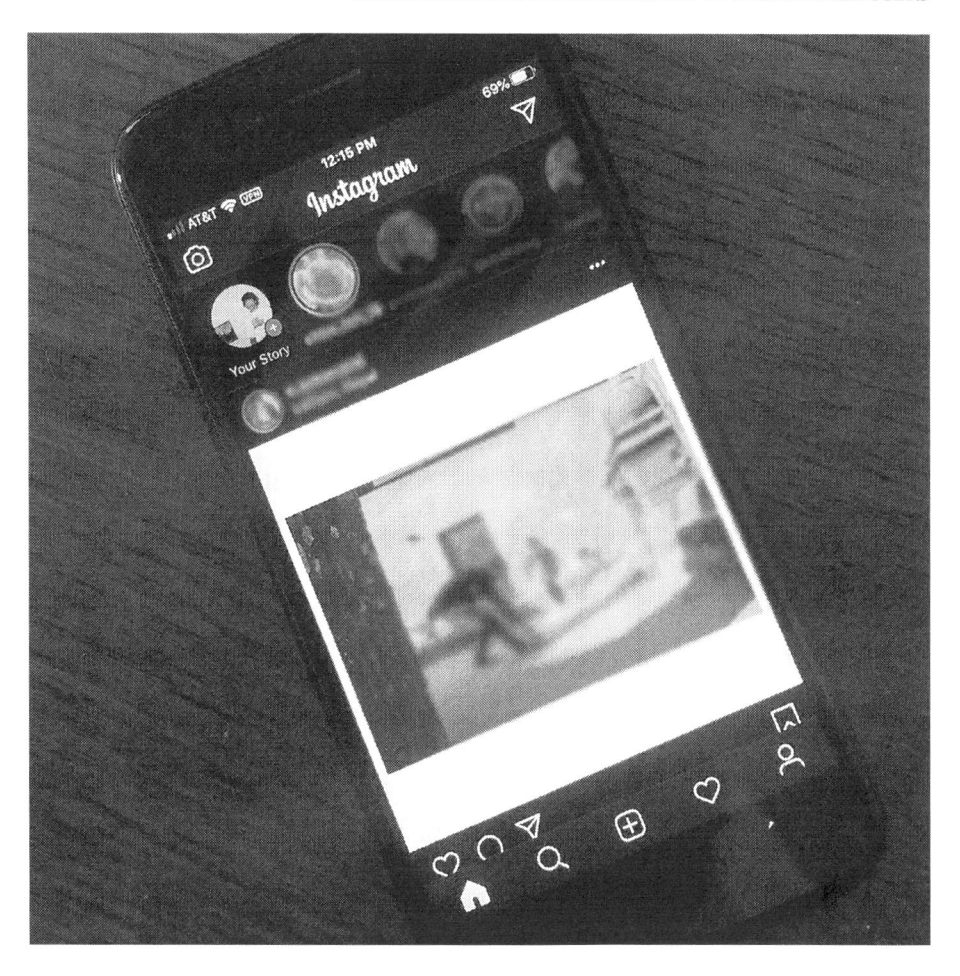

DISCLAIMER!!

Instagram is designed to be addictive. When you start getting more likes, comments and followers on Instagram, you will want more and more! So please proceed with caution, as I want you to grow your profile. But also please set boundaries so that this doesn't take control of your life! If you are a parent of a child who uses Instagram, please monitor their activity and set limits on the amount of time they use it.

After writing my thesis on Instagram, I learned from past research studies that people post for feedback-seeking. It could be conscious or unconscious, but that's the main driver for posting. This leads to issues, especially with young kids who are still developing mentally. They could develop problems with their identity, and the use of this and similar apps have lead to low self-esteem. Although it should be noted that these apps are somewhat new, so long term research is needed to learn the full picture.

Instagram displays the number of likes and comments on your photo. People may compare themselves to others and the infrastructure of Instagram allows users to do that. I strongly suggest parents to talk to their children about social media apps and tell them that these apps are not real life. Parents should also guide children in ways that they could build self-esteem without social media. Certainly apps like Instagram should be used in moderation. Even today, I find myself manically checking the app after a post to see how many likes I get. It is so silly but the app is designed for engagement and you can't help but wonder how 'popular' a post gets. As a human, it feels good to be liked, albeit through an app on a phone.

Social comparison is another problem that arises from use of social media apps. Users are constantly looking at the content of others, and seeing the feedback their peers receive. The quantitative data is readily available as the number of likes and comments are displayed next to every post. This can cause users to wonder why their content is not as 'popular' as others. For young people growing up, this constant comparision can hurt their growth and self-esteem. 'Why is this girl getting more likes than me?' From my thesis, this comparison can be problematic for young girls as more provocative content generally gets more attention, more likes and comments. The value of Instagram content is tailored to the eye-catching, and unfortunately sex does sell. Therfore, the association of numbers to posts is problematic for young people as Instagram can easily be seen as a popularity contest.

One good thing about seeing all the analytics of your posts, is seeing what does well and what does not. If you are trying to grow your page, it's good to see the type of content that your viewers enjoy. However, as many Instagram accounts with a large amount of followers can attest to, sometimes you might choose what you want to post because you know it will be popular instead of posting what you want to share with your audience. You can see this easily on model pages. All their swimsuit pictures will get lots and lots of likes. While a post about their dog is less popular. I go into this concept more later in this book about knowing your audience and staying in your lane. But at the same time, it shows that certain content does better that others, and it's important to know that. It is very important to talk to your child about this before they start using the app and to check in periodically. Naturally, humans want to get lots of followers and lots of likes, but unfortunately no one wins by getting the most views. And since children, especially aged 12-17, are constantly trying to fit in, meet friends and become their own person, the use of this app should be monitored.

Overall, if you are a parent with a child using social media, please talk with them. See how they feel when they post or see posts from others. Remind them that this is not a popularity contest, and remind them that who cares if someone gets more likes than you! A good point that I like to make is that there will always be someone better than you, with more likes than you etc. What matters most is that you are proud of yourself. Personally I think 'screen time' or time spent with a device should be limited for young people and this definitely applies to apps like Instagram as well.

Instagram is just an app. Just focus on your own page and your own set of values, and try not to compare yourself to others. We need to be in the right mental state in order to use this app, because as I said, it can be addictive.

Note, too, that these techniques are proven successful as of Spring 2020. Instagram is constantly evolving and therefore these techniques may have varying results in the future! Think about how different this app is now when compared to how it was when it started. Do you remember how users could only post square pictures in the beginning? Those days are long gone and hopefully there won't be many more large changes, but who knows! So your results may vary, but proceed with confidence. The basic techniques should not only be *good for Instagram in the future, but other social media platforms as well.*

About Instagram:

The Instagram app was launched on October 6, 2010 and is currently owned by Facebook. As of Spring 2020, there are more than 1 billion active users and this app has shown consistent growth for the past 5-6 years. Instagram is the second most engaged social media platform behind Facebook, and Instagram skews to a younger audience, with most of the users under 35.

Why do people use Instagram? Well, from my sociological research, people like connecting with other people. And Instagram is a handy tool to reach that goal quickly and easily. You won't see lengthy text, event notices, and other features you see on Facebook. Instagram takes the power of visual media (most often the photograph) and uses that to connect you with others. It's simplicity is what keeps it popular. If you post a picture, within seconds you can get feedback.

As with other social media apps, the users provide the content and advertisements pay the bills for Instagram. Instagram is free to join and you can only post content with your phone. You can log in with a computer to see the content of others, but you cannot post from your computer.

It should be noted that communication on Instagram is limited to likes, comments and direct messages. Human (in-person) interaction is more valuable and has much more clarity than communicating through technology devices and apps. In person, you can listen to the inflection of people's voices and can also observe mannerisms. If you send someone a message that says 'sounds good,' people could interpret it as sarcastic or even perceive your enthusiasm as lacking. I suggest adding an exclamation mark for positive statements, especially when you want to show people that you really like what you're seeing!

Please know that this interface can be confusing at first, but the more your practice the easier it will get it. Try logging into Instagram a few times a day in order to get comfortable. Poke around and familiarize yourself with all the features. People are often afraid of touching the wrong button or clicking the wrong thing. Trust me, tap away! A great way to learn is to do it yourself. Furthermore, there are great Youtube videos that will explain features to you and will show step-by-step instructions if needed. The great thing about watching videos online is you can stop and rewind to catch everything they say.

Like many social media apps, Instagram has seen many changes over the years to its interface, design and algorithm. While it's hard to stay completely up to date with the changes in Instagram, please realize that this information is accurate as of Spring 2020.

The Algorithm

An algorithm decides what content you see and who sees your content. In its simplest definition, an algorithm is a set of instructions that perform a task, much like a recipe. If you have ever used Google search, you have seen the magic of Google's proprietary algorithm displaying the most relevant results, catered to you. Generally speaking, if you are creating a personal account and interacting with friends and family, then you do not care about the algorithm as it pertains to growing your page and getting more followers. But the main thing to remember about the algorithm is that it is subject to change. Therefore take the information in this book (written in Spring 2020) as a general guideline, and it may be different when you're reading this. Writing a book about social media is tough because it is constantly changing and new apps are added regularly. In fact a few things changed while writing this book, and I will note them as they come up.

But for those people (such as business owners) trying to grow their page, the algorithm likes consistent behavior and likes when users follow certain rules. Instagram likes users who post at the same time every day, who post and engage with similar content to their own and who do not overreach the limits of Instagram.

There are daily limits to the amount of posts, likes, comments, follows etc. that you can do on Instagram. Here are some numbers (but please understand that these are rough estimates due to the fluidity of the algorithm).

Daily Limits
Unfollow: about 5 per day (any more and you might get blocked from using this function for a period of time)
Likes: 1000 per day
Comments: 175 per day
Direct Messages: 75 per day

Other restrictions
2000 characters in captions and comments
30 hashtags for a post
100 stories at a time
30 characters for an account name

Long story short: you should post and interact on Instagram, but only to a degree. These limits are needed to prevent spam, bots and general misuse of the app. If you go over these limits, expect to have your account limited and some features may be deactivated. Continued misuse and your account could be terminated. Proceed with caution and always do your research on current daily limits.

Let's Get Started

In order to get started, you should download the app. If you are on an Apple device, head over to the App Store. For Samsung users, you can download the app from the Play store. Search for 'Instagram' and hit download. Depending on your connection, this may take a few minutes. Please note that you can sign up for Instagram on a computer, but you can only post on a mobile device, and overall Instagram is made for mobile. The first time you open the app, it will ask you to 'Create New Account' or 'Log-in.' Tap 'Create New Account and enter your phone number or email. I suggest using an email as I do not like entering my phone number anywhere online due to privacy concerns. Next it says to add your birthday and then most importantly it says 'Change username.' Instagram will automatically select a username based on your email or your real name that you enter. What should your username be? If you plan on using this account for personal use, then choose any username name that you see fit. If you are trying to post content and grow your page, then you need to choose a theme for your account first.

The Instagram world is vast, and there are micro-communities for everything you can think of: yoga, weaving, music, travel, skateboarding, fashion etc. What type of content do you want to focus on? You can even find micro-niches within these same examples such as: hot yoga, basket weaving, jazz music, travel writing, skateboarding photography, vintage fashion etc. Big or small, know your theme and be proud to be a part of it! But be weary of going super-niche with your theme, as these techniques might not work. For example, if you are into barefoot snowboarding in Boise, Idaho, then maybe you should broaden your theme to just snowboarding. You want to be part of a community that has people in it! Search around Instagram to make sure there are tons of people that enjoy the theme of your choosing. If your theme is too broad, you may get lost in the shuffle, too niche and there might not be enough people to network with. This is where you need to do some research.

Once you pick a theme, stay in your lane. Imagine if someone starts to follow your page expecting golf content and they see a post about cooking or another topic. They may unfollow or lose interest! For a small business, this is easy for you as you have already chosen what to post about, which should be about your business.

Now that you chose a theme, it's time to choose a username that corresponds to that theme. My theme is street photography and my username is Unfiltered Photography. When trying to find a username, you will notice that many of the simple and clever usernames are already taken. You can get around this by adding underscores or numbers, or any other way to differentiate your username from other users. Is the username 'SupermanFan' already taken? Maybe try 'Superman_Fan' or 'SupermanFan123' etc. Your username should make it clear to others as to what type of content you will be posting. Take your time with choosing a username. Although you can change it later, it's best to start strong.

Use a keyword in your username to attract people. Try 'Snowboarder_Jim' or 'Yoga_lover' etc. By just looking at my username (stylized as: unfiltered_photography_), you have a good idea of what my content will look like. Furthermore, this is a strong username because as we grow our page we will be commenting on other people's accounts. Since my username has the word photography in it, other Instagram users assume that I am also a photographer. Therefore my username invites them back to my own page. For example, people may be intrigued at the validity of my comments and want to come to my page to view my work. Whatever your username is, the goal is to get people to check out your page and not just anybody, but people that might enjoy your content. Also, make sure your username is easy to spell and easy to search for. It should not be a challenge to find you on Instagram. For business owners, choose the name of your business or something similar.

After you select your username, Instagram will ask if you want to

"Find Facebook Friends' or to 'Find Contacts.' It's up to you if you want to use these features, but it's a good way to find people you already know. Next up is selecting a profile photo. Don't worry about this too much as this also can be changed at any time. But think of your profile picture as your logo for your brand, it should be a strong image or graphic. Eventually you may want a profile picture to reflect your content, but any picture of yourself is good for now. For business owners, use your logo.

Once you select your profile photo, Instagram will have a few other prompts about 'Discovering People' etc. Feel free to look at these and read on once you are ready.

The Interface

When you open Instagram via your mobile device, you will see a screen like this (with different content of course. Your Instagram is tailored to you and the people you follow):

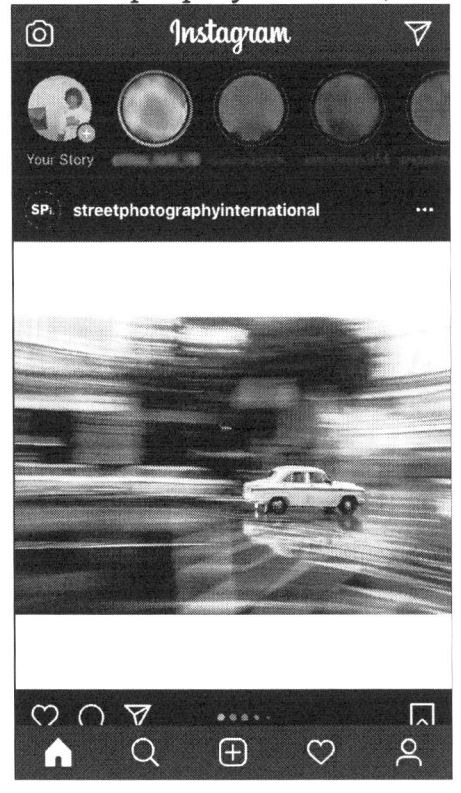

In the above screenshot, you see my profile picture in the top left and content from the people I follow is displayed on the home screen. (I repeat, your home screen will be personalized to you and you will not have the same content displayed as I do!)

This home screen where you see the content posted by the people and hashtags you follow.. The icon at the bottom will be highlighted when you are on that section of the app (notice the 'home' icon is highlighted here).

For example the heart will look like this when selected: ♥

Here are the other icons that you will see at the bottom of the app.

⌂ = home screen, here you can scroll and view content from your followers. You will spend lots of time here.

🔍 = the magnifying glass which is where you search for people, places and hashtags. Tap the search box at the top to get started

⊞ = where you post your own content to your page and for your followers to see

♡ = where you see who liked or commented on your page. This section is called your 'Activity'

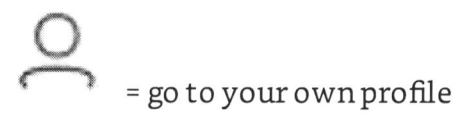

👤 = go to your own profile

As I mentioned above, the icon will be highlighted or filled in when it is selected.

A few more icons that I want to talk about are displayed on the home screen. As you scroll down on your home screen, you will see these icons:

♡ = tap this to like a post (you can also double tap an image to 'like' it

💬 = tap this to write a comment

✈ = (sometimes referred to as a paper airplane), tap this icon next to a picture to add the picture to your story, or send to a friend via a direct message.

Finally, on the far right there is a bookmark to save the post for later.

Underneath that you will see who liked the photo and underneath that are the comments on that photo. If you keep scrolling, this basic template will repeat and repeat. Also, below each photo you will see how long ago a person posted, which will come in handy later.

[Personal information has been blocked out]

Chapter 1 - Gather #Hashtags

The great thing about Instagram is that the app lives on your mobile device. We only need a few seconds to make a post. A few instances where you could post if you do not have tons of time include: waiting at the doctor's office, sitting in line at the grocery store, or walking your dog. These can all be opportunities for you to grow your page. However, please please please, be careful! I do not want you to walk into somebody or hurt yourself while using your phone. Use your phone safely when out in public! If your work/school commute involves sitting on a bus or train, then that would be the perfect time to grow your Instagram. Be creative and use those seconds and minutes wisely.

Now that you understand the legitimate concerns of using an app like this, let's find some relevant hashtags. A hashtag is a category within Instagram. If you click on one, you will be taken to a page where other photos are tagged with the same hashtag (on the last page, it shows what the screen looks like when you click on the hashtag #street_avengers for example). This feature is very important for our journey as hashtags are a great way to find people that have a similar theme to our content. Think of hashtags as categories where you can put your posts into. If someone is interested in a specific topic, and you add that hashtag to your post, it will be a great way to show your content to new people. Each hashtag is activated by stylizing the words with the # symbol (like this for example: #hashtag), and adding the hashtag to your post description or comment.

In order to get started, click on the magnifying glass icon at the bottom of the screen, tap the search box at the top, and select 'tags.' Search for some keywords associated with your theme in order to find some relevant hashtags.

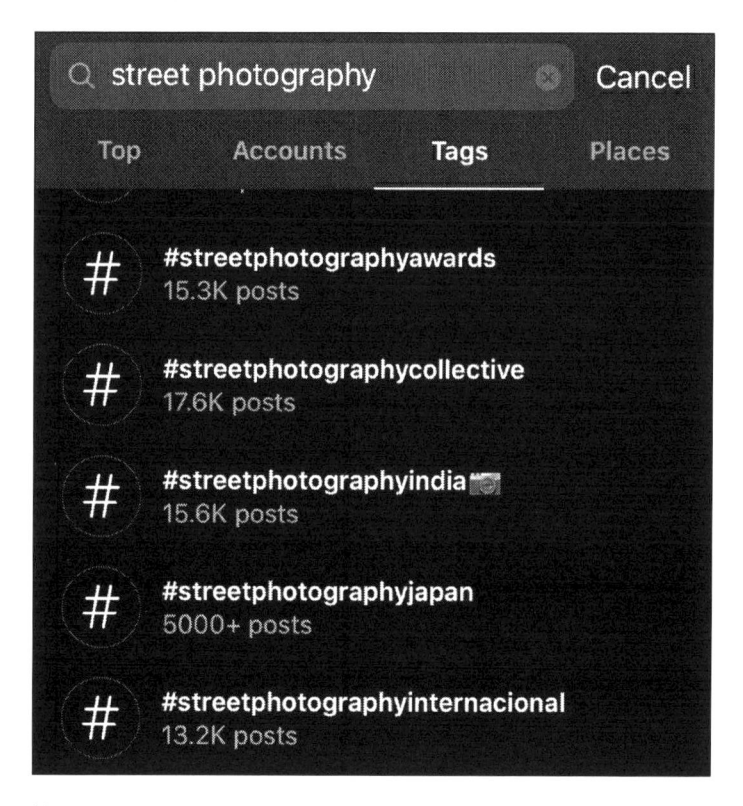

> **#streetphotographyawards**
> 15.3K posts
>
> **#streetphotographycollective**
> 17.6K posts
>
> **#streetphotographyindia**
> 15.6K posts
>
> **#streetphotographyjapan**
> 5000+ posts
>
> **#streetphotographyinternacional**
> 13.2K posts

Personally, I mainly use photography hashtags. I use a combination of 'feature accounts' (meaning accounts that feature other people's work) and tags of varying popularity. Hashtags with millions of followers may sound great, but many people post with these hashtags and your post may get lost in the shuffle! Smaller hashtags can be beneficial as the pace of posted content is at a more manageable rate. Both small and large hashtags have benefits.

In order to find out how big the hashtag is, click on a hashtag and refresh it to see if posts are getting 'bumped' down quickly. Look to see if new content is constantly being posted. It's hard to catch people's attention if the content is flying by too fast. If that's the case, the hashtag may have too big of a following. You are more likely to be seen on small or midsize hashtags after your post because there are less posts to scan through. For example, if someone searches within a small hashtag with less than 20,000 followers, your post has a better chance of staying near the top and therefore can easily be found. In general, find hashtags with large and small followings. Your results may vary, so use a combination of large, medium and small sized hashtags to find out what works best for you! For me, I use hashtags ranging from 50K to 1 million followers or more.

Protip: Check your spelling! Make sure you have the hashtag spelled correctly. If one letter/number is off it won't work! Also there should never be spaces in hashtags.

Once you find some good tags then you won't have to revisit this process for awhile. And if you want to go through this process quickly, find another profile in your theme and just use their hashtags for now, meaning copy and paste their hashtags on your own post. Furthermore, as of Spring 2020, you are allowed 30 hashtags on your post! You can either put these tags in the post description or as a comment (please note: recent updates to the algorithm in November 2019 led 'experts' to believe that listing 30 hashtags in a row could be considered spam-like in Instagram. Take some time to find the best hashtags and be prepared to switch them up from time to time. Try using less hashtags, like 10-15 if you experience problems (meaning you receive less likes and comments) with using 30. Switch it up until you find what works for you.

Besides searching or using the tags from another account, there are a few other ways to find hashtags for your theme. For one, you can do a Google search i.e. search for 'the best hashtags for (insert your theme here).' But please test the tags you find on websites as some may be outdated or obsolete.

Another way to gather hashtags that takes a bit more time, is to glean the hashtags from not one but a few different profiles that are similar to yours in content. This is a great way to find proven and relevant hashtags. Write down which ones they use, click on some to see how many followers they have and start choosing your favorites. Again, it's good to have a combination of hashtags, meaning collecting ones with a large following and some with a smaller following.

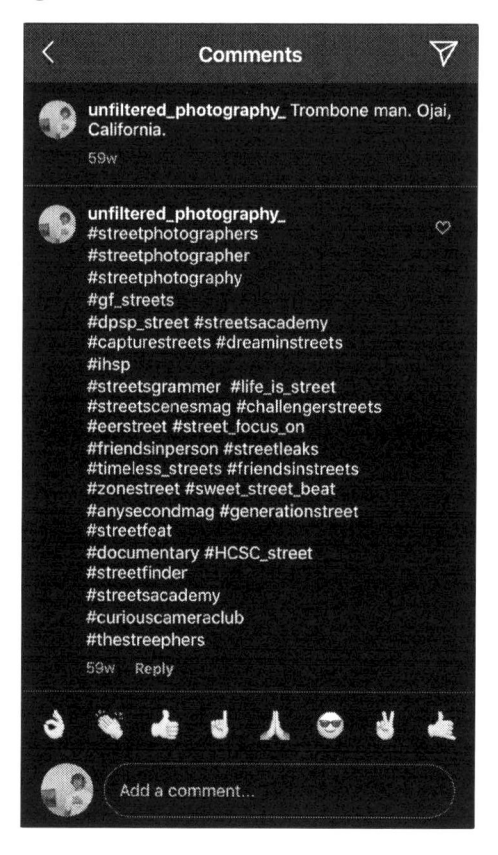

Ideally you want to find at least 60 or more hashtags for your theme and most certainly they should be specific to your theme. The idea of finding 60 is so that you have two groups of 30. It's always nice to mix it up, add more, swap out a few here and there, etc. It's good to change it up some times! Instagram seems to not like people spamming (i.e. posting over and over again) any of their features. Meaning you will be flagged for bot-like behavior if you do too much on the app at once or post similar words or hashtags over and over. Generally speaking, the algorithm likes when users use the app, but in a personal way with varying content (in summary this means appearing to be human in the way you use the app). Instagram will not like it if you post 100 pictures in a day and comment on 100,000 posts at once etc., anything that would be beyond the possibility of a human.

In appears that Instagram does not like people using the same hashtags over and over again, so please mix it up! Personally, I make two lists on my phone, so I can just cut and paste the hashtags. I'll use 30 the first day and the other 30 the next day. I'll swap a few out and eventually I'll have lists of many hashtags and rotate the ones that I use. Lately I have been experimenting with using 15-20 hashtags and it seems Instagram prefers users using less than the maximum of 30 hashtags. But feel free to use all 30 on a post to start.

Feel free to check in with other users and see what hashtags work for them. Once you become friendly with someone in your theme, this is a great question to ask them!

Another tip for hashtags is to log in to Instagram on your computer. This makes it much easier to find and save hashtags. Just copy and paste the hashtags you like into an email and then send it to yourself so you can have access on your phone. I can speak for most people when I say that it's much easier to copy and paste on a computer as opposed to a mobile device!

Pro tip: Find and utilize hashtags from other countries and in other languages. Instagram is worldwide and we can easily engage with people around the world! Take advantage of photography (and therefore Instagram) being the universal language! Google Translate is a great resource for translating words to other languages.

In summary, use 20-30 hashtags in each post with the hope that someone (that is not following you) sees your post via the hashtag, likes it and then follows your page. You do not always get results here, but if you have minimal time to dedicate to growing your page, this is step one. Generally speaking, we are trying to get people to notice us, and not just anyone, but meaningful people that will like our content and interact with us. Using 30 hashtags is a good first step. I like to put the hashtags in a comment, but some people put them in the caption. Try both to see what works better for you in regards to return on investment so to speak.

Chapter 2 - Post engaging content and eye-catching photos

Ok, we now have everything needed to make a post, except the imagery! Let's talk about posting pictures. I studied photography and I have worked as a photographer for many years. I have a more in depth photography section at the end of this book, but here are some basics.

Photography combines technical knowledge of a tool (the camera) and a creative eye. When trying to get better at photography, start by looking at examples of photography and other visual art. Choose whatever style interests you, I personally enjoy studying Renaissance art for the compositions. Studying the classics and other examples will help you engage your creative eye. Look at some famous pictures and art. What stands out most about this work? Also, there are lots of great photographers on Instagram But a word to the wise: if a page has thousands and thousands of followers, it does not necessarily mean that they have the best content.

Next, begin to study light, especially the direction, intensity and color. Start by looking at the shadows in the picture. This will help determine which direction the light is coming from. Take a picture in the same spot at multiple times of the day. Study these pictures to see how different the feel and mood is of the pictures depending on the direction and intensity of the light. Generally speaking, shooting in midday sun is not very flattering for people as there will be deep shadows under the eyes. Soft light is great for people, so try shooting portraits on a cloudy day. For displaying texture, side light is good. These are just a few examples. Shoot every day and experiment with light! By just holding a flashlight near a subject and moving it around, you can see how light and shadows change the entire picture!

Finally, know the camera and how to use it. Or not. It's important to know the guidelines of photography but also realize they are not rules, but only guides. Feel free to experiment, but overall, have fun shooting. My best advice is to practice every day.

Know that eye-catching imagery gets more likes. Find out what types of content your community enjoys and focus on posting similar content! For me, I take pictures of people in the streets and in public. A type of image that has been successful for me is one that is moody, simple to understand and may have silhouettes or interesting light. A complex image, or one with lots of small details does not work well. Keep in mind that the majority of users on Instagram are using a phone to log-in and therefore are viewing your imagery on a small screen! Make sure your photo reads well small, meaning it is easy to understand small. That is another limitation of this app, images appear small and you need to catch people's attention. Users scroll and scroll and it takes a lot for someone to stop and look.

We don't need to focus on just photography. Any type of digital visual art can be posted, including flyers, postcards, messages, texts etc. If you are into graphic design (and especially photography) then this app is perfect for your content. With the addition of stories, live videos, and IGTV, movement and sound add another layer of complexity for content creators.

So get used to posting pictures (or visual content) on your page! How often should you post on Instagram? Post at least once a day, twice at maximum. Along with posting engaging content with strong imagery, please ask questions, and/or write an interesting prose in the description. You want to attract people's attention and encourage them to leave a comment. Instagram loves when people use their app and interact with people. Writing an interesting description that engages other users is an easy way to attract attention. Instagram can be like a snowball rolling down the hill. It might be slow to start, but if you start posting daily you will see your following grow and grow. Try not to miss a day when posting. But overall, the more you comment and like the content of others, the more you will get out of it!

Protip: Besides using 30 hashtags in your post, add your location. People can find your post when they search for that city!

As for what time to post, there are varying schools of thought, and your results may vary. You certainly want to post during peak-use hours, and these may vary. As for Monday-Friday, I feel that 10am to 2pm is the worst time to post as people are at work or school. Usually 6 or 7pm works well or late at night, due to the fact that most people grab their phone first thing in the morning and we want to catch their attention at that time. Experiment with the timing and it may depend on your theme as well. The weekends are less predictable, but early evening seems to be the best time to post in general. One way to find out when your followers are online is to upgrade to a business profile. From there you can check out 'Insight' to see when your audience is online. For my account, it looks like most people are online each day around 9am. Feel free to upgrade to a business profile (it's free) to check out some of these analytics, but these are more advanced techniques.

Besides posting great content, you have to log in frequently. This sounds challenging; however, it could be just for a few moments when standing in line somewhere or sitting on a bus etc. The sole purpose of Instagram is to engage and interact with others. Therefore, feed the beast! This means, log-in, like photos, comment on photos, send private messages-it's time to meet and interact with people! You can spend as little as a few seconds to several minutes to converse with people, and it will benefit your growth. Connecting with your existing followers is an important aspect to growth. We want to keep your current audience engaged and not have them unfollow you. They will be meaningful followers, in other words, they are ones that have similar interests and interact with you frequently and we want to keep them around. What's great about meeting people on Instagram is that whether you are extroverted or introverted, you can do it! Although the current algorithm is shrouded in secrecy, it seems that Instagram likes when users post meaningful and thoughtful content, and Instagram likes users that interact with similar users.

Protip: Find some of the largest accounts that use your theme. What type of content do they post? What hashtags do they use? What accounts do they follow? It's good to learn from the best and mimic some of their techniques!

Chapter 3 - It's time to grow

Now let's meet people that may want to follow you. If you have a theme, let's find people that post similar content. If you are into salsa dancing in California, let's find other salsa dancers in California! The reasoning here is that people with similar interests as you will be interested in your content! This seems simple, but please stay in your lane. The general philosophy is to engage with people/accounts in your niche, and there are a few ways to do this. Let's focus on who we should target, which are meaningful followers.

The people you search out should have similar content to your own. Not only will you have a better chance of them following you, but you will want to follow them for inspiration! Networking on Instagram is much like real life. Show interest and cultivate the relationship. Just because you follow someone doesn't mean the relationship ends there. Like and comment on their photos and even send a personal message occasionally (especially when you really like one of their posts!) Be authentic and you will grow organically.

A quick note, there is lots of opinions and writings about Instagram and the best tips to grow. A few examples of tips include:
-posting at the same time every day
-posting only twice a day
-write meaningful captions and comments (as Instagram knows when your are being authentic or at least it tries to know)
-use good hashtags
-interact with others, meaning like and comment other people's content as much as possible

Long story short, I have heard many strategies when it comes to growing your page. Experiment on your own and find your own strategies that work best! Instagram changes the algorithm so much that it is hard to tell what works best right here and now without trying it out! At one point, your 'home' feed was in chronological order and now it's a mixed bag as to what content you see on your home screen. Sometimes I get picture after picture from the same person, with almost 70% of the content from the same user. The algorithm can be confusing, so trial and error works best to find out what works for you.

The definition of meaningful followers are followers who will continue to post comments and like your photos on an ongoing basis. In other words they are authentic. This is different than the bots and fake accounts that you can purchase online or followers you may get from ads. These types of users may be just be a number in your follower list and therefore are not valuable! We want people that are friends and that we can cultivate the relationship. We want to be authentic with our followers. This idea is much like real life, but keep in mind the communication is much different when using technology.

There are a few ways to find new friends and ultimately new followers. Keep reading for the ultimate secret in finding new followers. This may be the most valuable part of this book! The main way to meet more people and get more followers is simple: you have to meet people!

Do you have that list available with all your favorite hashtags on it? Great! Search for one hashtag, preferably one that has 300K followers or more. Once you click on that hashtag, click on the tab that says 'Recent'

This will show pictures that were posted most recently. Let's interact with people that posted recently, with the thought process being to get people to notice you (and what better way for them to notice you than when they are online and looking at their Instagram!) This will increase the chance that they will see you and interact with you. This is our ultimate goal, find people that might want to interact with you. This is one of the most important takeaways from this book when it comes to growth, interact with people that recently posted a picture with the assumption that they are still on Instagram, ready to see notifications from you about your likes/comments etc. In the most recent iteration of Instagram, by default, a notification will pop up on your screen when someone leaves a comment further helping your case on getting noticed!

Protip: Love Rihanna? Great, but unfortunately she probably won't be following you back. Any users with a tremendous following are not our targets here. We are trying to find people who enjoy our content and are willing to follow back. We want people who we can interact with and appreciate each other's content!

Look through the most recent photos posted a few minutes ago on the hashtag you chose. Find an account that aligns with your interests and with content similar to yours.

Now for the second best kept secret. It's time to get their attention. We know that they are online or were just online recently since they just posted (make sure to look at the time the photo was posted, we want someone that posted less than 1-2 minutes ago)

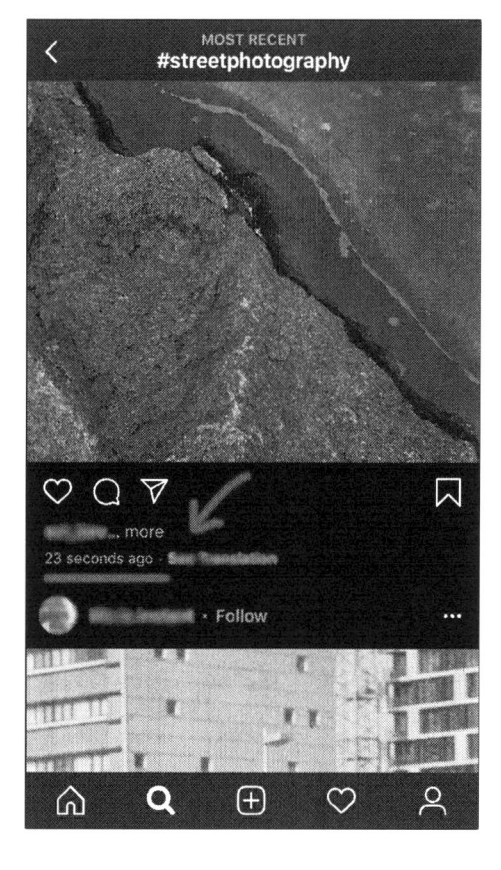

We assume they are still looking at the screen and we have to get their attention quickly. So comment with sincerity, meaning instead of posting a one word comment or emoji, ask questions and try to engage with them. Comment in complete sentences. As a photographer, I use questions like 'Where was this photo taken?' or 'What camera do you use' or 'What photographer do you use for inspiration?' The goal is to ask meaningful questions. Instagram is built to communicate with others, so let's communicate with others! But I make sure the comment is not generic. This means I will comment something specific about the photo such as: 'I love the light at that time of day. I was at that church a few years ago, it looks different!' These meaningful comments prove two things: 1. That you are a real person and 2. You took the time to admire their work in a thoughtful way. You are trying to engage with them and be authentic. You will learn that most people (even some of the big accounts with lots of followers) will write back or at least 'like' your comment. As humans we love feedback and recognition, so use this strategy to your advantage! You want to come across as genuine and not begging for followers, proceed carefully here!

Please note, recently Instagram does not place all the 'Recent' content in chronological order. I do not know why they changed that. You can still find people that posted most recently, but you may have to scroll down and look a bit to find someone that posted a few minutes ago.

Protip: This technique of engaging with people who just posted recently also works well with the people you follow! If I scroll through my home feed and see someone just posted, I always try to leave a comment. Getting attention and interacting with your current followers has value as well. Generally they will recognize your page and check out your photos! The world and technology move very quickly in this day and age. Therefore we have to be creative in how we get people to stop and take a look at us!

In order to build meaningful relationships and to hint at them that you want them to look at your page, I like to post a comment such as: 'You have inspiring work, I had to follow.' or 'Looking forward to seeing more.' And then I immediately follow their page. If you caught their attention, hopefully they will circle back to your page, like your content and follow you! I have much better luck saying: 'Wow what a beautiful photograph. I love the shapes of the windows and the light how it hits the ground at the perfect angle. How long did you wait for someone to walk through here?' vs. 'Great shot.' Also, there are profiles that spam posts with generic responses. Let's stand out in the crowd and overall Instagram loves when people have conversations on their app. Open-ended questions instead of yes/no questions (or no question at all) will take you further here! Try to engage with them in a thoughtful way. Engage with purpose! Everyone is different, so results may vary but this is the very basic strategy to finding followers. And we are not finding just fluff, meaningless followers, but authentic followers that want to see your content and will interact with you in the future. Find those people, engage with them and invite them (in a genuine way) back to your own page. Nobody wants someone to spam 'follow me!' a thousand times on every post. Instead, make an honest effort to engage with someone and they will want to check out your page. Genuine and thoughtful comments lead to genuine relationships. These strategies reflect real life!

To summarize this technique: Find a user that doesn't follow you on Instagram + engage with them with likes + add a few meaningful comments on a picture or two + see if they respond by visiting your page + follow them if it seems they like your page or invite them to do so!

Here is a scenario that comes up a bit: you check out your likes/comments and the potential follower recognized your comments and writes back! Make sure to respond to them. Then exactly what we want to happen, the person is now on your own page liking images. This is a goal, get the person to come back to your page. Continue to interact with them and hopefully they will follow, but please don't be discouraged as not everyone will follow at this point. Maybe make another comment mentioning how great their content is and that you 'had to follow.' The goal here is to show how genuine you are and that you followed because they had great content! I repeat: not everyone follows back so don't get frustrated! In conclusion, we are employing the technique of 'follow for follow back,' however instead of directly asking or begging, we are suggesting it by our actions and doing it in a more casual, less forceful way.

Protip: Find accounts with a higher number of 'Following' vs. 'Followers.' This tells me that they will be more likely to follow you. If the account has tons of followers but doesn't follow many accounts, don't try to get them to follow you. Most likely they only follow a few select folks and are too big of a page to care about following someone back! The ratio of following vs followers is important! Please view the screenshots on the next page.

vs.

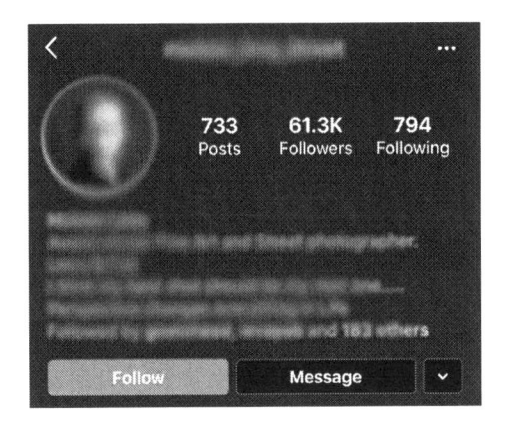

Most of my followers I have never met in real life. However, I would consider many of them to be my friend. They have given me advice on what camera and lenses to buy and even had people give me personal advice. Instagram is an amazing tool to connect people. From my sociology thesis, I determined that people love to connect with people and Instagram is just a tool in helping with that in 2019 and beyond.

But I hear you guys, can't you just buy followers? Yes you can and you can quickly get 'fake' followers for a price. This book is about gaining meaningful followers and spending $0, so I won't suggest it here. Also, people can quickly tell if people bought followers as there is 5-10% likes/comments compared to their number of followers. (i.e. they have 100K followers and their posts get only 100 likes). Also, these will not be valid followers and you won't be able to engage with them (sometimes referred to as bots). It's a quick fix but not a good option in my opinion. You can also buy a bunch of likes for one post, but what about your next one? Or what if you buy a bunch of followers and only a fraction like your posts? A better option would be to share your Instagram profile on other social media platforms i.e. Facebook and try to interact with humans. Tell your friends to follow you! If you have real followers, you will receive more likes and comments. If you buy fake interactions, you will get fake results.

There are multiple ways to find people on Instagram. One technique that I recently tried was by tapping the 'search' icon (magnifying glass) at the bottom of the screen. This takes you to the Instagram 'Explore' page. Scroll down through this section, as Instagram recommends photos that you might like here. Although the accounts in this section are of varying size (meaning they might not respond if you comment), it is still a good way to find people similar to you.

Another method is that I like to look through my followers and look at the comments on one of their pictures. Anyone that is active on Instagram, and is interacting with others (i.e. posting comments) may want to interact with you! If you find a user that made a great comment, click on their page! They probably won't be online right then, but if you find someone who makes meaningful comments then they would be a good candidate to follow you!

One other technique is to scour your favorite hashtag. Anyone that posts with a hashtag that you use probably has similar content. However, I have found it easier to find people and get their attention if we know they are online (meaning they just recently posted an image). Use these or other techniques, the most important tip is to find people that might be interested in your content and that have a strong chance of following you. If you follow someone, and they don't log-in to see until hours later, they could easily miss that notification.

Protip: Pages that are great to follow include at least one of the following:
1. a user with similar content to yours.
2. a user that recently posted a picture (less than 2 minutes ago).
3. that follow more people than have followers (ratio imbalance)
4. overall you see them responding to feedback on their page (i.e. responding to comments on their posts).
5. that have liked/commented on one of your photos.
6. People you know in real life

In summary, find profiles of people that have similar content. Get their attention by engaging with them right after they post (by checking the 'Recent' tab of a hashtag or seeing when they posted). You can do this by liking and posting intriguing comments with substance. Establish a back and forth relationship and hopefully they will come back to your page to follow you! I also have the word 'photography' in my username, so hopefully this gets their attention even more, by showing them that I am a photographer as well.

At the end of the day, you want to drive traffic back to your page, and this is my main strategy for finding meaningful followers. But feel free to find other techniques that work for you! For example, I visited a photography messageboard before (or sites like Reddit) and created a topic about Instagram. I got a few new followers that way, but feel free to think about other ways to find new people.

Protip: Once you befriend someone, ask them if they want to do a shout out for a shout out. Meaning, ask them to repost your image or give you a shout out and you will do one in return! This will expose your profile to their followers and hopefully steer them back to your own page! Foster those relationships! The 'Stories' aspect of Instagram is great for this. Look for pages with similar or slightly bigger follower count than you so it can be mutually beneficial.

So the above is a great technique in finding more followers and growing your page. I recently came across another tip to consider. Step one, go to your profile and click the three horizontal lines in the top right of the screen. Scroll down to where it says 'Discover People.' On this screen you will see a list of people that Instagram thinks you might want to meet and follow. Generally these are users with similar content as you. Recently I have visited this part of Instagram and visited a few of these profiles. Many will have a similar or smaller number of followers as you do. I would say that at least 75% of the people featured here are worth checking out! Like a few posts, make a few comments and see if they take notice. It's a great idea to let Instagram do the hard work of finding accounts to follow. They usually suggest similar accounts so feel free to check this out!

If you do all of the above in regards to meeting people you should be getting new followers! It all depends on the time you spend. Make a goal to engage and try to get at least 1-2 followers every time you log on.

Don't be afraid to send private messages as well. A month ago, I saw that one of my followers posted a photo from the same spot I had shot a few months ago! I sent them a message and I was like 'Wow I was just there, such a cool spot!' We started a conversation and eventually the person wanted to see the picture(s) I had taken in that spot. I sent them the photo and they posted it on their story! It was a great interaction and this goes to show that meeting friends leads to meaningful relationships, which leads to more followers!

Another quick story: a photographer from Spain has been following my page for awhile. Just recently he gave me some good feedback about my images. It was the perfect constructive criticism and I really took it to heart because I enjoy their content. It was a pleasant surprise, but one you can only get from a meaningful follower. Sure you can buy ads or buy followers, but they could be just numbers on a page, this book is about getting followers that are valuable, proven here with my Spanish friend (someone I have never met in real life) who gave me great advice. He was authentic, and those are the people we want to follow us!

In conclusion, to compare this app to real life, consider a 'like' to be like waving to someone to get noticed and a 'comment' is when you actually talk to someone. Both can be valuable in the virtual world but commenting (like the real world) will always be more valuable. The only drawback is that it takes more time to write a comment. Also, if you spend more time with who you engage with instead of trying to interact with as many people as possible, you will have better results (less is more). When trying to get lots of attention quickly, I call this the 'spray and pray' method. Consider this similar to shouting in a public place. You may meet some people but you will not be perceived as authentic and you may scare some people away. Instagram, in this way, is much like real life. If you want to meet people, you need to engage them in a thoughtful and honest way.

Chapter 4 - Use your time wisely/ authentic followers are important

I grew my page from zero to more than 1800+ followers quickly with these techniques. I used only a few minutes a day! If you don't have lots of time, then these tips are for you! Spend a few minutes at a time just here and there. The flexibility of the phone and this app means you can grow your page anywhere at any time (as long you have a signal and a charged phone). Please don't ignore your friends or family or real life obligations just to achieve your goal! Log onto Instagram when it makes sense, when there is downtime. I do not want this app to negatively affect your life.

If you are asking about if you only have a few minutes a day, what should I do? Here is the breakdown: click on a hashtag, look at the recent posts and look for new people to engage with! Within a minute, you could comment and like multiple posts from one specific user, and casually invite them back to your own page. But there's a fine line here. Do not like every single one of their photos and do not post absurd amount of comments. A rule of thumb is to like 5-10 photos and make 3-4 comments on photos when reaching out to a new user. If you do not like typing on your device, features such as Siri (or Bixby on Samsung) can turn your speech into text!

Protip: What would it take for a 'stranger' on Instagram to get *your* attention? For me, they would have to make some genuine comments or ask an intriguing question. Employ this idea when approaching others. Authenticity, although more time-consuming, wins.

That being said, Instagram likes users that engage with others, log in frequently and post engaging content. Just scrolling through your feed does not engage with others. Use your time wisely, meaning make a point to at least meet someone new each time you log in. Write a lengthy exposition with your picture (2-3 paragraphs), invite people into a discussion, ask questions and reply to each comment. Instagram rewards people that use the app as intended. They also reward people that use the app on a daily basis, multiple times a day. This is due to their complicated algorithm, no need to understand it but realize that they like people using their app frequently! Make sure to respond to every comment, to show that you are genuine and appreciate the time they took to comment.

I've noticed that if I take a break from the app for a few weeks and then make a post that not many people will 'like' it. Once I start posting every day again (regardless of the merit of the photograph), each day I will get more and more eyes on my page! It's a mystery as to what content gets put onto your homepage feed (i.e. what you see from others). So be persistent, but keep in mind that daily users are better for Instagram and better for your own growth.

On Instagram, you do not need lots of time to be productive in growing your page. If you have…….

0-30sec = open the app, like photos on your feed, comment (as time allows), respond to comments

1-3min = search a hashtag, find a potential follower, like/comment on their page. Write a comment to the effect of 'looking forward to seeing more' or something similar, casually inviting them back to our page.

4min or more - combination of above +
Post a picture, find new hashtags, meet people etc.

Chapter 5 - Feed the beast

Wash, rinse, repeat! Engagement means just like it sounds, engaging with others. These techniques are simple to learn, and just takes a few minutes out of your day. How much you want to grow depends on you and the amount of time you want to take. Although you might be thinking, I'll just post a comment or two on tons and tons of pages, surely they will all follow back! The more the better! In reality, less is more and keep in mind this is not a scientific method. You may engage with someone for days, they could like and comment on your page a bunch and they still won't follow you. On the other hand, you could try the spray-and-pray method, meaning make a bunch of quick comments/likes on many many pages! You may get a few people to follow you back but trust me, spending a little extra time engaging with people in a meaningful way will lead to a much more beneficial 'online relationship' than more random, happenstance encounters. Again, would you follow someone if they just liked one or your photos vs. someone who took time to write two meaningful comments and one intriguing question and like 4-5 of your photos?

Protip: Follow everyone back that follows you in the beginning. This shows good karma and shows people that you enjoy people that look at your page (because you're inspiring others to do the same!)

In conclusion:

-find accounts similar to yours (and ones that might like your content)

-engage with them and casually invite them back to your page. Please don't say 'follow me, I follow back' but instead be authentic say things like 'you have great work, worthy of a follow' or 'I can't wait to see more.'

-Make specific comments about the photos that show that you are a real person and are interested in their work!

-Comment on the details of the photo, use specifics like 'I love the color on her dress!" This way it shows people that you are authentic and took the time to take a look! Just like real life, people want to interact with people that are real and not fake.

On Instagram, tons and tons of people are trying to grow their own page. You will see lots of generic 'great shot' or 'nice' comments. But the difference to my technique is to go slow and really be particular about who you try to interact with. Stay true to yourself, make real and engaging comments and the followers will come! Spending a few minutes to give thoughtful feedback on one or two pages is worth more than spamming 'great shot' to dozens of users in the same time period. We are trying to grow your Instagram in a meaningful way so please be meaningful in your interactions!

Take your time, meet people and you will grow your page. I casually spent a few months with this and grew to 1800+ followers. I know this is not a very large number, but the only thing that was holding me back is my time. And the good thing about Instagram, it can reward you for using the app. A user that opens the app frequently each day to comment and like pictures, is rewarded by having their posts shared with more people. Therefore if you use the app in a healthy way with a healthy mindset, you will achieve success.

Once you have created your profile, send me a private message on Instagram and I will follow you back! Find me on Instagram:

unfiltered_photography_

Chapter 6 - The 'Stories' feature, IGTV and the future of Instagram

These techniques are current as of Spring 2020. Please remember that these may become less effective in the future. This app has changed and may change again! It may also lose relevance and another app may come along (who here remembers Myspace?). That being said, these tips can help engagement on most social media platforms.

A question I get sometimes is about stories and videos. Like Snapchat, Instagram has a feature where people can post short video snippets and posts that disappear after a period of time. Please use stories as needed, it's a great place to promote a new post. It's also a good place to show people more about your personal life. Stick to your theme with your posts, but on your stories feel free to show more about you! A post about you getting a new job might not be good as a post, but could make for a great 'story.' I'm not a big fan of stories, but watch a few stories from other accounts to see what you think. Many people use them so feel free, they are definitely gaining in popularity. Think of 'stories' as a different way to engage with your audience, try it out! Recently, Instagram added even more ways to customize your stories with texts, links, polls, filters etc. My suggestion is to hit the paper airplane button ◁ next to your post, and select share to story. This way, anyone that sees your story can click on it and it will direct them to your profile.

IGTV is a newish video feature that is not as popular as the other features on Instagram. Users can post videos up to 10 minutes and stream live as well. It's great that Instagram offers options for video, so use this feature if it can benefit you and your niche.

Finally, there could be more new features added in the future, so please test and use them in a meaningful way. Instagram is just a form of communication and with technology, the methods and ways to communicate are constantly changing! It's always good to read current news and articles to hear what experts say about the Instagram algorithm and look for other tips to grow your page.

Glossary of Terms

Algorithm - a fancy word for a scientific equation as to how and what content is show on your feed. Think of this as a recipe or a process that is created to generate an output. In this case, your interactions on Instagram leads to how much (or little) your content is promoted.

Bots - a non-human that can perform automated tasks (such as spamming likes/comments, following many pages at a time or other various tasks used to increase engagement through automated means. Instagram tries hard to feature human accounts. The less bot/inactive followers you have the better

Business profiles - you can 'upgrade' to a business page and you should if you want to really control marketing strategies, and take advantage of the analytics that Instagram provides. There is not much of a difference between personal and business accounts. But with business accounts you can see analytics of your followers, posts and overall have access to valuable data for marketing purposes. Go to Settings>Account to 'Switch to Business Account' on Instagram.

Comment - similar to other social media platforms, add a message to a post so the user can see it and respond! This is a great way to interact with users that you want to follow. Between a like and comment, a comment is more valuable and can be more authentic.

Emoji - a small icon, picture that helps with communicating via text. Some popular emojis are the smiley face, thumbs up and heart icon. You will see a ton of these in the comment sections of Instagram. Great for impersonal communication but it is quick.

Facebook - at one time, the king of social media, now seeing some decline due to public controversy due to Facebook's privacy policies and questionable business dealings. Facebook owns Instagram. One of the most ubiquitous apps and even websites worldwide.

Feed: similar to Facebook, if you press the 'Home' icon within the app, a feed of photos from your followers, hashtags that you follow and ad's will appear. Most users spend their time here.

Follow/unfollow - you can find this button on every page. If you follow a user, their content will appear in your feed and they will be notified that you followed them

Filter - once a defining part of Instagram, now is less of a defining feature. However, many filters are offered and can be used to alter an image - from simple black and white conversion to adding more contrast. Consider using a filter or filters consistently to make your content more exciting or visual stimulating

Hashtag - a fundamental part of Twitter and integral to growth on Instagram, the # sign is a great way to connect you with other users on Instagram as well. Consider hashtags like categories or topics. Place a #hashtag in front of the text with no spaces.

IGTV - upload videos up to 10 minutes long. This is not the most popular feature of Instagram, but could be another handy way to interact with others.

Like - double-tap on a post or click the 'heart icon to show that you approve of the post. This is the most basic way to interact with other users on Instagram. As of 2019, there has been discussion to remove or limit this feature as experts fear this can lead to low self-esteem and a false sense of identity and self worth. As I wrote in the disclaimers in this book, activate a healthy relationship with Instagram and log out when feeling addicted

Personal message (DM) - these messages are private between two users, much like an email but within Instagram. DM stands for direct message.

Private vs public accounts - If you are trying to grow your Instagram, public account is the way to go. However, think about going private for your personal pages. And to all the parents out there, please make sure your children's social media pages are on private.

Snapchat - similar to the 'stories' feature of Instagram, this social media app made the 'short videos that disappear' function popular. It is still seeing a steady amount of users.

Stories - just like another social media app Snapchat, this feature allows users to post quick videos, additional info and content in a post that disappears after a few seconds. Use filters, icons, text, music and other features to jazz up your story.

Spamming - this word means to repeatedly post/comment/engage and can be borderline harassment. Computer created tools and programs are made for spamming, however real people can do this as well.

<u>Twitter</u> - Social media app that focuses on text blocks, once defined by limiting to users to 140 characters. Now users can use up to 280 characters for their posts. Popular with breaking news.

Basic photography tips

I've been a professional photographer since 2005 and I am a former photojournalist as well having worked at *The Free Lance-Star* in Virginia among others.

The biggest photography tip I have is to shoot more! Take pictures every day! I'm not a better photographer than you, I just have taken many, many more bad pictures than you have.

Lighting - Without lighting, photography does not exist. Start looking at what direction the light is coming from and how shadows change with the time of day. The light from the sun at noon looks much different than the light at sunset. Also ask, is the light diffused, or hard and direct? Look at the shadows on a cloudy day vs. a day with open sun. If you start identifying what type of light you are shooting in, you can begin to use it to your advantage. For example, if you are shooting a landscape photograph or a subject where you want to show off the texture, try shooting with light from the side.

Another tip with lighting is to understand the difference between the human eye and the camera. The camera can only see a fraction of the range of light that our eye can. Have you ever tried to take a picture of someone next to a campfire? You can only expose for the fire, or the person, not both. (this is why your flash automatically goes off, to try and fill in the light). Your camera can shoot the bright highlights OR the dark shadows. It will not register both. Are you shooting inside? Get creative, turn off the overhead lights and use a lamp to illuminate your subject. Move the lamp around and notice how the shadows change. A trick of a trade is to put a plastic bag or transparent sheet in front of the lamp to diffuse the light. BE CAREFUL THOUGH! Some lamps get hot and the bulbs can melt or ruin what is put near it.

There are tons of books out there on lighting, but these were some basic tips. Study light and understand the difference between what the camera and human eye can see. The camera can see (and expose for) just a fraction of the light and shadows that the human eye can distinguish. You can take a picture of the shadows OR highlights of a scene, not both.

Composition - I could write a whole book about composition. A good place to start is to look at the elements of design: color, shape, form, lines, texture, value and space. Learn about each one of these. And a good way to practice is to choose one of these elements and spend a whole photoshoot focusing on that element. Most great photographs use multiple elements in one picture. I also suggest studying classic paintings like ones from the Renaissance period. Look at how they place their subjects and other elements in their paintings. A few other compositional ideas to research are the rule of thirds and the golden ratio.

Also keep in mind that photographs are 2D. However, we can use tricks such as putting elements in the foreground, middle ground and background to achieve depth. This will help guide the viewers eye through the photograph as well.

One final note about composition, although you can crop the photo after you take it, I like to frame my pictures in my camera so there is very little cropping done in post. Try to get the photo right the first time. Editing is great to fix minor things in your photographs, but it should not be used as a tool to save a poorly composed image.

Backgrounds: Another good photography tip is to watch your backgrounds. I see amateur photographers do this all the time, they find something to photograph, their dog for example. They will take a picture of their dog, usually from 10-15 feet away and within that photograph there will be rocks, car in the foreground and a bunch of trees, signs etc. in the background. To take better photographs, exclude, exclude, exclude. This means that once you choose your subject, make sure every element in the frame helps to accentuate the subject. If not, crop it out. Either physically take things out of the frame or move to a place with a better background. Sometimes getting down low can clean up a messy background (see the next section on 'Different camera angles.')

This is not to say that a messy background cannot work in a photograph, but I'm saying that generally you want the background of your photograph to complement the subject of the photograph. I feel that just looking at the entire frame and making sure all the elements work together, will turn your snapshots into frameable photographs.

Different camera angles: We have all seen the world from our eyes, and photos from our standing height are usually boring.

What does the world look like from above, or maybe your dog would look cool if you got on your stomach and shot from the ground? Experiment with different angles. One of the best pieces of advice for me was, 'make the ordinary, extraordinary." Show the world in a new and unique way! Photographs that make the viewer asks questions are more valuable than ones that are straight forward and show the world from an angle we all have seen. Use the camera to show the world your unique vision.

The Decisive Moment: A term used by the legendary street photographer Henri Cartier-Bresson. Photography is great for capturing moments, and by using a camera you can capture an instant of time. Look for the peak action or the smile on your subjects face. A great moment ALWAYS makes for a great image.

Color/black and white/filters (toning your images)
First off, please study the color wheel in order to learn about which colors work well together. This will help you when you are out shooting.

As for toning your images (and when I mean toning, I mean adjusting the light/shadow areas, the color, the contrast, etc.), your smartphone and Instagram itself has a few options. Phones are getting very advanced with photography and you can easily crop and edit/tone your photos right on your phone. Tap 'edit' when you are looking at a photo on your phone to see all the options.

At the basic level, you can use an Instagram filter for your photographs. When you post a picture on Instagram, the second screen it takes you to (after you select the image you want), is a menu where you can select a photo filter. Try a few to see how it changes the mood of your photograph.

If you feel comfortable, you could also take your photo into Photoshop and really do some creative editing! There are lots of resources out there, but please try to be consistent with your style. It would be great if your images were consistent in theme and style so your photos stand out, and creating consistent looking content will help grow your page (and keep your followers engaged). If the color of a photo is bland or does not help support the idea of your image, try changing it to black and white. Black and white photography, with its absence of color, will highlight shapes, form, lines, texture etc.

Cell phone tips:
These photography tips are with the smart phone user in mind. You surely can take pictures with a 'professional' camera, but there will be more steps to your workflow, and those lessons are

for another book! When using a digital camera, you will have to get those photos from your camera to your phone (in order to post on Instagram). Some fancy cameras let you send the photos to your phone via bluetooth, but overall if you use a digital camera you will have to add another step to your workflow, which is using a computer to import and export the photos. There is no right way to create content, but realize that it may save time to keep the whole process on your smartphone. Meaning, at the beginning, take photos on your smartphone and within seconds you can upload that same photo to Instagram. This is that fastest workflow as of now.

But the great thing about using your smart phone camera is that you can shoot many photos. You are only limited to the storage space of your phone You are limited in not having precise manual controls (unlike a professional camera), but the phone cameras are getting very user friendly and phone cameras are becoming very professional tools for photography. For one, on new iPhones there is a 'Portrait Mode" which helps to blur the background and makes the photo more professional. The 'Night Mode' is great for low light situations. Feel free to do more research about your specific phone as they are getting to be very versatile with photography. You probably know that feature length movies are being shot on iPhone, so be thankful that your are holding a powerful photography tool in your hand! Overall there are tons and tons of features with cell phone cameras, feel free to watch a tutorial or read more about your specific phone.

❖ ❖ ❖

Thank you for reading, please reach out via email any time: ctwehling@gmail.com

CHRISTOPHER WEHLING

Book edited by Andrea Howry

ABOUT THE AUTHOR

Christopher Wehling

Christopher has a degree in Photojournalism from the University of Missouri-Columbia and a degree in Sociology from Webster University. His thesis about Instagram included the most current research as to why people post. Currently, his Instagram has grown to more than 1800 followers, by only using the strategies in this book. Christopher only spent a few months growing his page, so your only limitation is your time! To learn more, please visit his website at: ctwehling.com

Printed in Great Britain
by Amazon